I0813170

AMAZING ART FORMS

The Art of Music

BY CANDICE RANSOM

Kids Core
An Imprint of Abdo Publishing
abdobooks.com

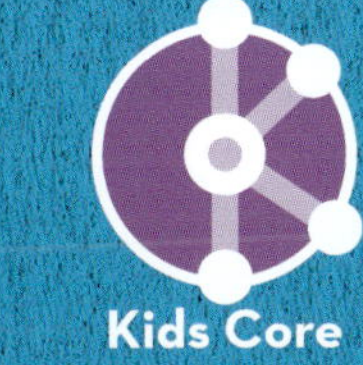

abdobooks.com

Published by Abdo Publishing, a division of ABDO, PO Box 398166, Minneapolis, Minnesota 55439.

Printed in the United States of America, North Mankato, Minnesota.
102024
012025

THIS BOOK CONTAINS RECYCLED MATERIALS

Cover Photos: Shutterstock Images (guitar, amp, background)
Interior Photos: Rea Nakalelo/Shutterstock Images, 4–5; Orion Production/Shutterstock Images, 7; Shutterstock Images, 8, 10–11, 12, 22, 24, 28 (bottom), 29 (top); Jeremy Chan Photography/Getty Images Entertainment/Getty Images, 15; Olly Curtis/Future Music Magazine/Future Publishing/Getty Images, 16; Three Lions/Hulton Archive/Getty Images, 18–19; Bettmann/Getty Images, 21; Gareth Cattermole/TAS24/Getty Images Entertainment/Getty Images, 23; John P. Kelly/The Image Bank Unreleased/Getty Images, 25; Cheangchai Noojuntuk/Shutterstock Images, 27; Yalcin Sonat/Shutterstock Images, 28 (top); Xavier Gallego Morell/Shutterstock Images, 29 (bottom)

Editor: Haley Williams
Series Designer: Katharine Hale

Library of Congress Control Number: 2024938373

Publisher's Cataloging-in-Publication Data

Names: Ransom, Candice, author.
Title: The art of music / by Candice Ransom
Description: Minneapolis, Minnesota: ABDO Publishing, 2025 | Series: Amazing art forms | Includes online resources and index.
Identifiers: ISBN 9781098295776 (lib. bdg.) | ISBN 9798384916772 (ebook)
Subjects: LCSH: Art--Juvenile literature. | Music--Juvenile literature. | Musical Works--Juvenile literature. | Music industry--Juvenile literature. | Music and society--Juvenile literature. | Art--Technique--Juvenile literature. | Arts and history--Juvenile literature.
Classification: DDC 781--dc23

CONTENTS

Recorders have seven finger holes on the front and one thumb hole on the back.

CHAPTER 1

Making Music

James was helping his mom clean out the attic. In one of the boxes he found a long, wooden musical instrument. He gave the instrument to his mom and asked what it was.

"My recorder!" his mom said. "I haven't seen it in years!"

James's mom placed her fingers on the recorder's holes and put the mouthpiece between her lips. She then blew a short breath. As she blew, she lifted some of her fingers. Different sounds floated into the air. James knew the **tune**. It was "Twinkle, Twinkle, Little Star."

"Everyone in fourth grade had a recorder," his mom said. "Our teacher taught us to play." She handed the recorder to James. He held the

Bird Bone Flute

In 2008, scientists discovered a hollow bone in a German cave. The 40,000-year-old bone was from a bird. It is about 13 inches (33 cm) long and has five round holes. Scientists believe the bone is an ancient flute. They think it may be one of the oldest musical instruments.

Music stores sell a variety of instruments in different sizes, shapes, and colors.

instrument like his mom had. His mom pulled a book out from the box. “This was my old songbook. I can teach you how to play.”

James was excited to learn how to play the recorder. He wanted to make different sounds float through the air. He wanted to make music.

A choir is a group of singers who perform together. Choirs may sing during religious ceremonies or in musical competitions.

What Is Music?

Music is a form of art. It involves creating many sounds using instruments or people's voices. These sounds can express feelings or ideas.

Experts believe that human voices made the first musical sounds thousands of years ago. Early humans may have sung songs. They also made instruments to create music-like sounds. They may have banged on rocks or blown into seashells. Some also used parts of animals to create musical instruments.

Music comes in many forms. One person or a group of people can create music by singing. People can also make music electronically or with traditional instruments. Music is said to be a **universal** language. People around the world enjoy listening to and making this art form.

Further Evidence

Look at the website below. Does it give any new evidence to support Chapter One?

Music

abdocorelibrary.com/art-of-music

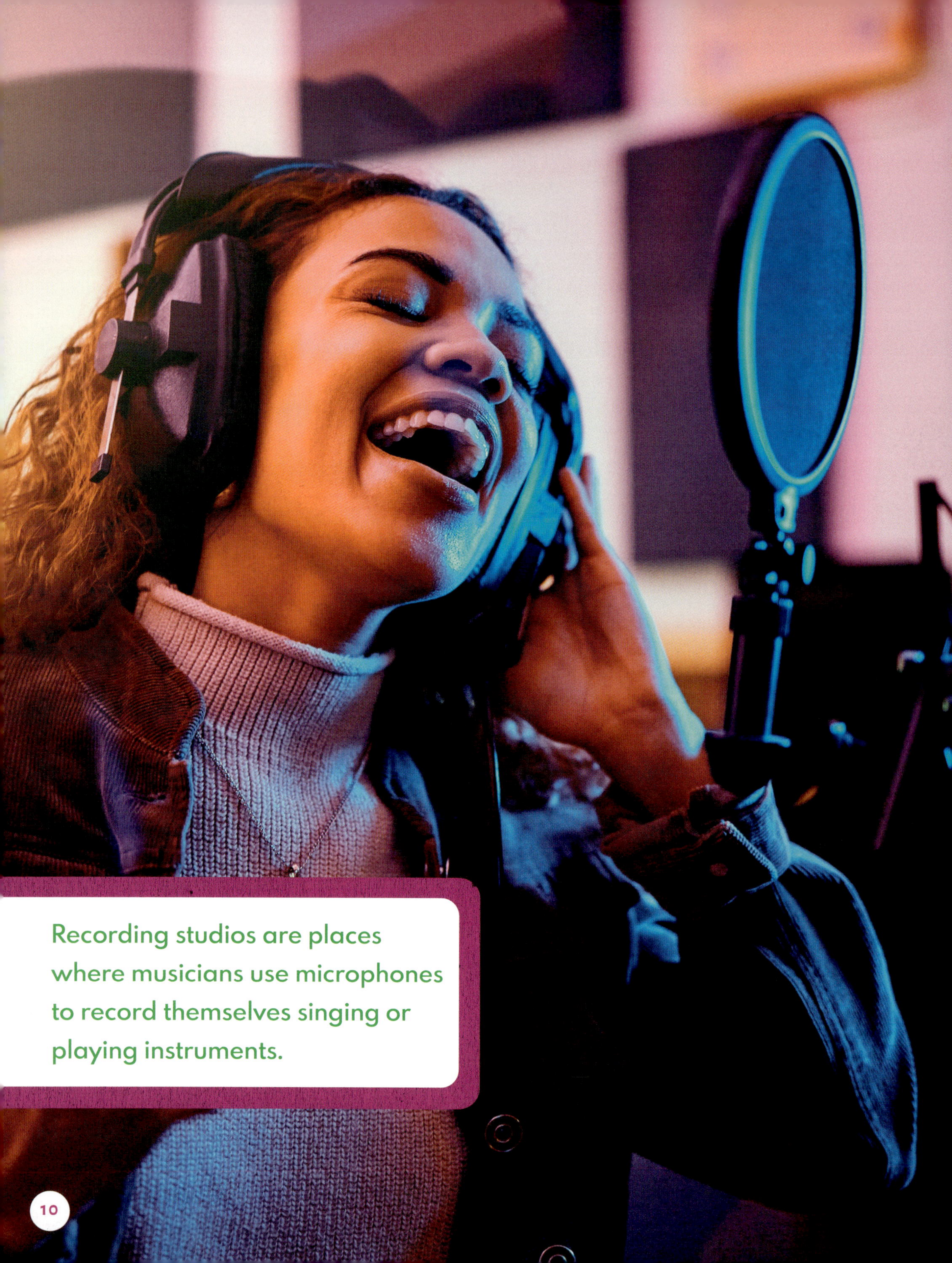

Recording studios are places where musicians use microphones to record themselves singing or playing instruments.

CHAPTER 2

Music Basics

Music is sound. Sound moves through the air to people's ears. Musical sounds are different from noise. Noises are usually random and unpleasant. But musical sounds are arranged in a certain way. These sounds are created to be pleasing to people.

Sheet music has symbols on it that tell a musician what notes to sing or play.

Elements of Music

Different elements combine to make music. First comes musical notes. A single note is the smallest part of music. Many notes put together create a song. These notes each have a different pitch. Pitch is how high or low the note sounds.

Notes organized in a pleasing way create a melody, or tune. Harmony is when two or more notes or sounds are played together.

These sounds can come from people or instruments. Songs also have rhythm. This is a pattern of short and long sounds. Rhythms often repeat or form a steady pattern. This is called the song's beat. Beats can be fast or slow. For example, strong and fast beats are usually found in dance music. Beats help form a song's tempo, or speed.

Writing Songs

For many years, people sang songs that were not written down. These songs were learned and passed from person to person. Eventually, songs were **composed** by people. They were written down using a system of symbols. The symbols show which musical notes to sing or play. This system is called notation.

These different elements come together to create the form of a musical piece. A form can be as simple as one person singing a song. Or it can be a **symphony** being played by many instruments.

Musical Instruments

Many forms of music are made using musical instruments. Today, there are four main types of instruments. They are string, woodwind, brass, and percussion.

String instruments have strings that create sound. These include violins, guitars, and harps. The sound is made by **plucking** or rubbing the strings. Woodwind instruments are hollow with a mouthpiece at the end. This allows musicians to

Large musical groups called orchestras perform concerts using string, woodwind, brass, and percussion instruments.

blow through them to make a sound. Common woodwind instruments are clarinets and flutes. Brass instruments are curved, metal tubes that are wide at one end. One example is a trumpet.

A music synthesizer is a machine that can electronically create and change sounds.

Musicians also blow into brass instruments to make sounds. Drums and gongs are percussion instruments. These instruments must be hit to produce sounds.

Some musical instruments use electricity to create sounds. Electric guitars and pianos are connected to speakers to increase their sound. Computers also make music. Some people use a computer to **compose** songs. It can also be used as a digital musical instrument.

Virginian Dena Jennings makes banjos from **gourds** she grows on her farm. Enslaved Black people from Africa originally brought banjos to the United States. Jennings talks about the importance of the banjos she makes:

> I cannot get enough of the banjo. It has been a real link to the music I heard as a little kid.

Source: Amber Galaviz. "Jennings Finds Music, Medicine Share Healing Properties." *Daily Progress*, 5 Aug. 2020, dailyprogress.com. Accessed 29 Jan. 2024.

What's the Big Idea?

Read this quote carefully. What is its main idea? Explain how the main idea is supported by a detail.

Many musicians today still play Ludwig van Beethoven's famous piece Symphony no. 5.

Music around the World

There are many types of music. Classical music is formal. Austrian Wolfgang Mozart and German Ludwig van Beethoven were two famous classical music composers. They created symphonies during the late 1700s and early 1800s.

Operas are performances that use live music to tell stories. Chinese opera is an ancient tradition. It uses singing, dancing, music, and costumes to tell a story. Important events in Africa are celebrated with drum music. The drums are made from wood, metal, or clay. Different sized drums have higher and lower pitches.

Several types of music come from the United States. Enslaved Black people created a type of music called the blues. Jazz music came from the blues and marching bands. One jazz musician was Duke Ellington. Country music began in the southern and western United States. These songs often tell personal stories, such as Loretta Lynn's "Coal Miner's Daughter."

Jazz musician Louis Armstrong, *middle*, was famous for his trumpet playing and singing skills.

Music for the People

Music that is enjoyed by many people is called popular (pop) music. In the 1950s, singer Elvis Presley became one of the first rock and roll music stars. He is often called the King of Rock 'n' Roll. In the early 1960s, the British band the Beatles created fun and catchy rock songs.

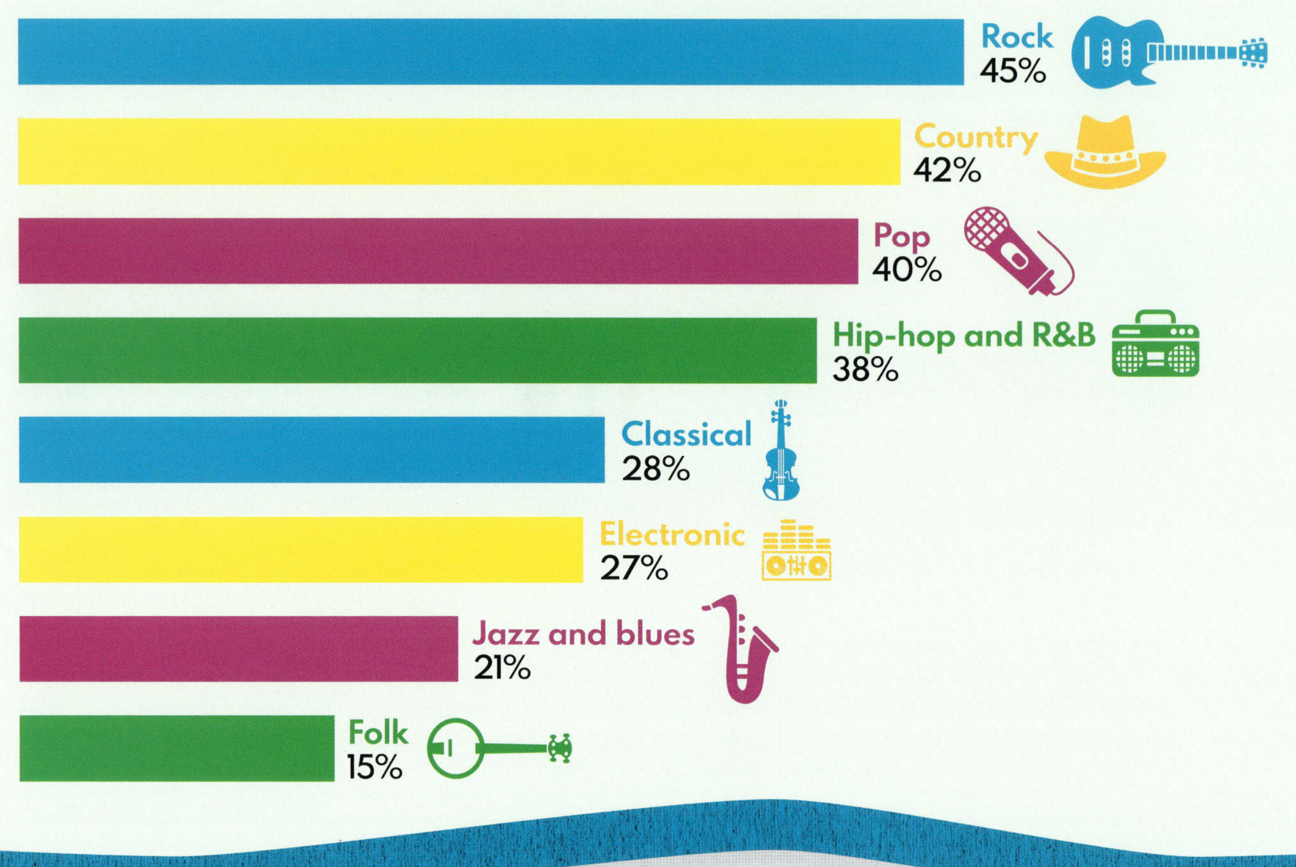

From July 2022 to July 2023, more than 9,000 US adults were surveyed to find the top music genres they listened to.

Taylor Swift began as a country music singer and songwriter. She eventually switched to singing and writing pop music. Today, Taylor Swift is considered one of the biggest stars in

Taylor Swift performed in more than 150 shows around the world for her Eras Tour.

the world. She has won many awards for her music. Her songs and albums are often featured at the top of music lists.

BTS is a popular boy band from South Korea. The band blends different styles of music with Korean-pop, also known as K-pop. K-pop usually involves both singing and dancing.

The Sydney Opera House sits on Australia's Sydney Harbour. It took 14 years to build.

Music Venues

There are many famous music **venues** around the world. Carnegie Hall is located in New York City. People go there to hear classical, jazz, and

The large rock walls on either side of the stage at Red Rocks Amphitheatre help carry sounds during concerts.

pop music. Australia's Sydney Opera House holds a variety of musical performances. In Colorado, people can listen to outdoor concerts at Red Rocks **Amphitheatre**.

Many people enjoy going to music festivals or concerts. Some music fans attend the Coachella Valley Music and Arts Festival in California every year. There are also museums related to music. The Rock and Roll Hall of Fame Museum is in Cleveland, Ohio. Visitors can go there to learn about the history of rock music.

Music is everywhere. People can create it with their voices. Or they can use musical

Woodstock

In 1969, one of the most famous music festivals was held on a farm near Woodstock, New York. The festival was called Woodstock. It was held from August 15 to 18. Thousands of people went to listen to many popular bands and musicians.

Smartphones, radios, computers, and music players are some of the many devices people can use to listen to music.

instruments to make sounds. However it is performed, people around the world enjoy listening to and making music.

Explore Online

Visit the website below. Does it give any new information about jazz music that wasn't in Chapter Three?

What Is Jazz?

abdocorelibrary.com/art-of-music

Art Supplies

Pen and paper for writing songs

Voice

Sheet music
Instruments

Glossary

amphitheatre
a curved outdoor performance space

compose
to write or create a work of art, such as a song or poem

gourds
hard-shelled fruits related to pumpkins

plucking
pulling and releasing a string quickly

symphony
a long piece of music for many kinds of instruments to play together

tune
a specific series of musical notes

universal
something that occurs everywhere

venues
places where events are held

Online Resources

To learn more about music, visit our free resource websites below.

Visit **abdocorelibrary.com** or scan this QR code for free Common Core resources for teachers and students, including vetted activities, multimedia, and booklinks, for deeper subject comprehension.

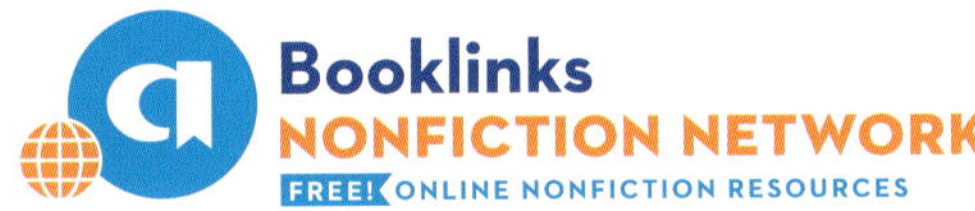

Visit **abdobooklinks.com** or scan this QR code for free additional online weblinks for further learning. These links are routinely monitored and updated to provide the most current information available.

Learn More

Abdo, Kenny. *Pop Music History*. Abdo, 2020.

Gieseke, Tyler. *Percussion*. Abdo, 2023.

Richards, Mary, and David Schweitzer. *A History of Music for Children*. Thames & Hudson, 2021.

Index

About the Author

Candice Ransom has written many books for children. She still has the recorder she got in fourth grade and can still play "Twinkle, Twinkle, Little Star" from memory.